T0065461

EDUCATION IS POWER!!

A COMPARATIVE ANALYSIS OF PERFOMANCE AND LEADERSHIP OF PUBLIC SCHOOLS VERSUS PRIVATE SCHOOLS IN TWO SELECTED SCHOOLS

Dr. Sabelo Sam Gasela Mhlanga

WESTBOW
PRESS®
A DIVISION OF THOMAS NELSON
& ZONDERVAN

WestBow Press books may be ordered through booksellers or by contacting:

WestBow Press
A Division of Thomas Nelson & Zondervan
1663 Liberty Drive
Bloomington, IN 47403
www.westbowpress.com
844-714-3454

ISBN: 978-1-6642-2510-7 (sc)
ISBN: 978-1-6642-2511-4 (e)

Print information available on the last page.

WestBow Press rev. date: 02/24/2021

CONTENTS

CHAPTER FIVE

LIST OF TABLES

LIST OF FIGURES

DEDICATION

This book is dedicated to my Princess, Sinqobile Shalom Gasela Mhlanga, the girl power and beloved wife, Judith and our four children Qhawelenkosi Blessing, Sinqobile Shalom, Thandolwenkosi Prosper and Nkosilathi Emmanuel and Joseph Nkosana and also to my dear late mother Josephine and late father Joseph Gasela-Mhlanga. In the same vein, the dedication goes to all teachers both for public and private schools who sacrifice their lives rise the standards of all students from various backgrounds. All children have a right to education regardless of their social backgrounds. The world would be a better world if all children in the communities are given a chance to education for all to reach their God's given potential.

Children are the asserts for today and for tomorrow and the investments in their education is an investment to the future generation. To all children out there, the future is in your hands and strive to be a responsible citizen and lift up your country, your community and your society by pursuing your dreams with integrity, respect, dignity and aspirations to change the world to be safe haven for all humanity. With our five children who are still budding, it is my wish to inspire them with hope and a brilliant future together with the rest of children in the world and assure them that with education they can touch the sky. The whole world is counting on the education of the children regardless of where they are. The girl-child in most of the third world countries do not have access to education because of their gender. The children, regardless of gender, ethnicity, race or nationality, they deserve and have to the rights to acquire education they need as an empowerment of their future. This book is dedicated all children in the entire world because education is power. May the Almighty God keep us together and protect us to change the world for a better place for all our children.

ACKNOWLEDGEMENT

The author is indebted to the following people for their invaluable contributions to the success of this book. My supervisor Mr. Mangwanda, a lecturer in the Department of Education, Master's program at Zimbabwe Open University, for his thorough and constructive criticism at each stage of this book. He was patient but committed and imparted to me research skills that I will use in my longevity. Rev. Andrew Muchechetere, my dear friend, Cephas Ngarinvhume, Rev. Alfred Simango, United Baptist Chairman and Dr. Bishop Joshua N. Dhube, United Baptist Church Overseer for their support and encouragement. The students and staff at Phoenix College and Hatfield Girls High schools for their cooperation in answering questionnaires and the interviews conducted, honesty and thoroughly. My beloved wife, Judith for assisting in extracting and compilation of the data from questionnaires and interviews. This was mammoth task. Finally, I wish to convey my profound gratitude to my family, Gasela Mhlanga and friends for their moral support and for accepting to be deprived of their attention and fellowship that they would normally have with me. To all United Baptist Church in Harare North and South, thank you and may God bless you all. To God be the glory and praise forever.

ABSTRACT

This research study sought to compare the performance and leadership styles of public school versus private school in two selected schools in Harare. The students' and teachers' views and perceptions of critical issues were considered.

The study used the survey research design. The major instruments used to collect data were questionnaires and interviews. A total of 132 students got the questionnaires and 46 staff got the questionnaires from Phoenix College and Hatfield High School. 60 students from Phoenix College returned the questions while 67 students from Hatfield High School returned the questionnaires. 21 staff from Phoenix College returned the questionnaires while 30 staff from Hatfield High School. The data collected was analyzed using tables, composite bar graphs, line graphs and pie charts.

It was established that each school runs its affairs in a manner that suits it. At Phoenix College the leadership / administration runs the school as a business entity and the performance and pass rates are higher than that of Hatfield High School at 'O' Level which is a government school.

This study revealed that most of the private schools are well advanced in terms of leadership / administration, performance compared with the public schools. The major differences are the incentives, benefits, allowances for teachers and academic resources and hardworking student. The research study posed a challenge to both students and staff to improve their commitment and work in order to record a land mark in education circles during their era. The Ministry of Education also was challenged to re-evaluate their policies, curriculum and execution of their work in order to meet the global educational standard. Further study is required to determine the best ways of improving both students and staff's welfare, conditions of service, remuneration, education resources and benefits in order to produce the best results.

CHAPTER ONE

Background to the study

There are numerous researches that have been done on Public Sector Schools and private Sector Schools in the entire world in general and in Zimbabwe in particular. However, the research did not give substantial comparisons of performance. In Zimbabwe, there are few researches that focused on the public schools with comparison in terms of performance with the private schools and their administration.

Most of the researches focused on Healthy, Development of Civil Society, Local Government, employment Creation, Law and Order and many others. The public sector schools are those controlled and run by the government. The private sector schools are those owned, controlled and run by private organization, companies, churches or individuals. However, the syllabus, curriculum and examinations are controlled by the government. Basically, public means the citizens of a particular country as they participate in political and social processes. "Public action is not just a question of public delivery and state initiative. It is a matter of participation by the public in the process of social change" (Muytt Mackington and Hewitt, 1997:4)

This comparative research study entails to investigate the truth about the performances of the two sector schools to determine which one performs higher than the other. The administration of the private sector schools seems to own the schools and their destiny hence record the success stories. The public sector schools seem not to own the schools, the administration move with the instruments from the Ministry of Education, hence the personnel do not own the schools and the destiny, hence, poor performance. The personnel have very little to contribute in the system hence redundancy of work. As the social benefits are widespread to the society from both sectors, there is, therefore, need to examine the best ways to achieve the objectives of each sector, so to speak.

The main thrust of this research study is, therefore, to compare the performances of the two-sector school, public and private, in regards to administration and students. In the private sector school, it has been argued that there is much innovations, creativity, pro-activity, result oriented, better working conditions, more incentives and benefits than in the public sector schools. Performances of both the administrations of the schools and the students will be compared critically, to promote efficiency, effectiveness and achieve better results in the education system in Zimbabwe. The questions such as poor performance in the public schools will be examined and high performance in the private schools will be critically investigated.

Statement of the problem

It has been assumed that the private sector schools' performances by both the students and administration record the higher performance in terms of results, standard, quality, efficiency and effectiveness in their deliverance systems compared with public sector schools. Although it is the mandate of the public sector, the government, to deliver social benefits and social goods to the society, it has been found wanting. In the private schools, there is minimum control from the government, there is transparence, motivation through incentives, more allowances, benefits, good condition of service and security, teachers are allowed to be creative and innovative, which ultimately promote high performance and good relationships. There is staff development. They work within their budgets as they are really in control of everything hence it promotes progress, whereas in public schools, the administration is tied up with government rules and regulations.

In public sector schools, huge financial resources are spent extravagantly and they channel the resources to wrong areas of their interest instead of the areas of need. The management of funds is very poor. The government does not give attractive benefits and incentives to their employees hence poor performance and low standards. This research study, therefore seeks to make a comparison between private sector schools and public sector schools. The comparisons will reveal facts that would be taken into consideration in order to improve the performance of public sector schools and further improve the private sector schools. Both from public and private schools, their facilities, infrastructure, stationery, textbooks and the welfare of the students and staff will be compared, so to speak.

Purpose of the study

The purpose of this research study is to compare the major reasons for public sector schools and private sector schools differ in terms of performance and the administration. Why there is underperformance of the administration and students in public sector schools, while they have the bulk of resources in terms of financial resources and material resources. Description and explanation will be given in the research study as to the major reasons of failure by the public schools to deliver high performance by both the students and the administration. The research intends to find out as to why the private schools perform so well most of the time compared to public schools.

The comparisons of two sector schools will determine the hidden instances of successes in private schools and underperformance of most of the public schools. The other researches that have been done, so far on this topic, do not clearly give justifiable reasons as to why the private schools record higher performances, most of the time, compared to public sector schools. The results will, ultimately reveal and unveil the major reasons of the differences. The gaps with other research studies that have been conducted will reveal the intricate secrets and then possible solutions to curb the major differences be sought, in order to enhance the education system in Zimbabwe.

Sub-Problems/ Research Questions

The research study seeks to compare the following:

Are there differences in performance between private and public sector schools?

What are the differences in leadership styles between private and public schools?

Are there any ways to improve the condition of service to both the administration and non-academic staff?

To what extent does private sector school's administration foster progress, facilitate high performance and best results?

What are the major reasons for the public sector schools to under-perform?

What is the difference between the children who attend public schools compared with children attending private schools?

Significance of The Study

The study is worth pursuance, as it will provide the major reasons as to why the private sector schools thrive higher than public schools in terms of performance in administration and student's body. This research will assist the Ministry of Education, Education Policy formulators to be more relevant as to the needs of the students and the staff in respective schools. The government will be well aware of the plight and the challenge that are faced by its employees in terms of the conditions of service, facilities and infrastructures and staff houses. The companies, organizations, church and individuals who own private schools will benefit as they will learn as to what makes the private schools successful, most of the time. The stakeholders from both the private and public schools will examine and explore factors, which make one school better than the other.

Since this study is evaluator and comparative in nature, it will show the extent to which the stakeholders who are the beneficiaries see the research as achieving its objectives. The research study will bring to attention the policy makers to take cognizance of factors that can slow progress, success, higher performance, efficiency and effectiveness. The research will reveal areas of weaknesses and then improve the education standard to enhance the access to disadvantaged citizens. Both the government departments and other ministries and also the private sector will benefit to see the gaps that have been omitted by other researchers. The public schools will discover the loopholes and gaps and be able to improve, promote progress and high performance.

The curriculum and syllabus formulators will utilize this data about relevant and sound education. They will update their systems and be able to review, revise and plan for quality education to enhance education system in Zimbabwe as long-lasting investment. The research study will reveal the areas of concern, to the educationists, to improve the modalities in order to provide the best education in Africa and beyond.

In the areas of staff development, the research study will outline detailed measures on how staff can be developed in order to deliver the best results and how to motivate the staff terms of delivery of good incentives, good benefits, good working conditions and allowances, better packages. The scholars will be able to examine the facts about this research study and follow up the perceptions, ideas and data established in this study. It is imperative for this research to deserve recognition in education fraternity because it endeavors unveil the grey areas, gaps and weaknesses in public sector schools compared to private sector schools. It will improve the interventions in educational sector.

This research study is aimed at assessing and evaluating government's structures and procedures and putting the resources where it is due. Cost-benefit analysis to both parents and students will play a pivotal role to let both the parent and child to decide which school to go to, public or private school. It is therefore, fundamental to read this research study, analyze it, deduce and implement the relevant concepts and ideas necessary in order to develop education policy and structures that will enhance education system in Zimbabwe.

Assumptions

The study assumed that:

The two sector schools private and public will be able to provide a fair and honest information to the researcher

Responses from two respective school administration and students are correct and given in good faith.

Information will be honest, accurate and relevant, as the researcher will hold interviews and give questionnaires to honest people.

Definition of Terms

Public Sector schools	-	It is the government owned school, which are run and controlled by the state
Private sector school	-	It is privately owned school run by either an organization, church, company or individual.
Performance	-	Act or process. It is execution of a duty to its logical conclusion.
Education	-	It is defined as a systematic instruction in the development of character or mental power
Economic growth	-	It is the growing of the Gross Domestic Product (GDP) and Gross National Product (GNP) of a country
Brain Drain	-	It is loss of skilled personnel by immigration
Standardized –scores	-	Percentages/ scores that conform to standard

Policy   -   This is a formulated course of action, adopted by a government or any organization, business or individual.

Justification   -   Organization or society founded for a particular purpose

Investment   -   To put money on a safe monetary institution to produce dividends. You invest property or individuals to get a return at a later stage.

Social Benefits   -   It is favorable or helpful factor, bringing advantage to the society or public. The ultimate purpose of any education system is not simple to produce educational out products and value-added but to generate longer term benefits, both individual and the society.

Infrastructure   -   These are basic structural foundations of enterprises for example roads to the schools, bridges, sewers etc. regarded as the country's economic foundation.

Autocratic   -   Absolute ruler. Dictatorial person without consultations

Authoritative leadership   -   is power or right to enforce obedience, delegated power, influence based on recognized knowledge or expertise.

Democratic or participatory   -   leadership favoring social equality and consultation of others ideas and suggestions

Delimitations of The Study

This research study will focus on the performance of private sector school versus public sector school in terms of administration and student performances. The research study will be done on two schools i.e., private school and public school in Harare urban. The study will not focus on all the staff and all the students in these two respective schools but will zero in few individuals within the two schools. The study will not address other issues outside areas of disciple of students, their expectations and their contributions and their contributions towards achieving better performance and leadership styles.

Limitation of The Study

This research study is purely an academic research, which might encounter a number of resistances as similar researches have been done by the government officials who are already biased towards education systems in existence. As a matter of fact, there are some teachers who are pro-government who might not be willing to disclose and reveal the truth about performances in their respective schools of research study. The researcher, therefore does not have the mandate or authority to force the respondent to honestly answer the questionnaires.

However, questionnaires which keep the respondent anonymous will alleviate this problem. The time and resources are not available for the researches while it would have been ideal to involve more than two sector schools i.e., private and public, in order to get the wide range of information about our education systems in Zimbabwe. The research will not be practically evaluating both the staff and students in their areas of work i.e., examining students in class or staff assessing their performance per se but it will be in a form of interviews and questionnaires.

Organization of The Dissertation

This first chapter has started the problem being studied and its facets. The research study questions were posed, insuated by the objectives of the study, the purpose and the sub-problems. This was followed by hypothesis, then the significance of the study and the assumptions. The definition of terms, the delimitation and the limitation of the study subsequently followed, so to speak.

In Chapter two, a literature review will be given with the relevant literature on two sector schools, i.e., private and public. The related literature by other authors will enhance this study. This chapter will be more informative in regards to the subject or topic by other authors. The public and private school's administration will be discussed and compared and the possible procedures that can render the best performance and good quality education.

Chapter three will deal with the research methodology, which will be presented. The research design and methodology look at how the public and private schools operate and how they differ in terms of their performance. The administration of both public and private schools will be discussed in detail.

Chapter four will present, analyze, interpret and compare data using the instruments explained in Chapter three. The data collected by means of questionnaires and interviews will be used to answer the questions raised in Chapter one. The chapter will make a comparison of performance between the two sector schools.

Chapter five which is the last chapter will be a summary chapter with conclusion and recommendations in the education system about how the public sector schools can improve and achieve high performance from both the administration and the students. The major findings of the performance research or private and public sector schools will be summarized then proposals be made in order to have efficiency, effectiveness, motivation and high performance in the schools for better future. Both sector school's performance will be outlined and to map the way forward will be given and possible solutions be suggested and encouraged to this subject matter.

CHAPTER TWO

Review of Related Literature

Introduction

This chapter reviews the literature available that has been researched on performance, leadership styles in both private and public sector schools. Poor performance in public schools has necessitated the research study to be conducted in comparison to the private schools. The research study will assist both the students and the staff in any given school to improve their performance. The pass rate in public schools seems to be lower than in private school. This research study therefore will zero-in on the performance between private and public schools, the leadership styles that might be contributing factors to low high performance and school administration in the world in general, Africa and Zimbabwe in particular. The reasons for underperformance will be revealed in this chapter, the incentives of the school staff will be looked at, critically and Education system in Zimbabwe, whether it is relevant to the current global change in education system. A summary of the chapter will conclude the chapter.

Performance Differences Between Public and Private Schools (World Schools)

a. British Education System

The government in United Kingdom sets out its core principles and values underlying reform. They bring in delivery mechanism that are responsive to what parents and students require, meet the needs of all. The core principles or values that education of Britain aims to achieve are:

Equality: Opportunity for all means that no reform must leave out any group. "Our vision of a school system which values opportunity for all, and embraces diversity and autonomy as well as the means to achieve it: (DFES, 2001:6). The style of leadership is democratic and freedom to exercise skills and to determine your destiny in terms of performance. Part of promoting equity means that educational standards must be raised in areas where they are correctly too low.

Autonomy: To achieve opportunity for all and to raise educational standards, the government reforms must promote diversity and autonomy. Autonomy (Private schools), is valued so that well-led schools take full responsibility for their mission. Autonomy is about enhancing freedom, so that educational entrepreneurs can successfully succeed. Private schools in Britain are given freedom they need to excel and innovate. In private sector schools, the government does not control, there is no autocratic leadership but are given autonomy to function according to their missions and visions. The British government has 'the White Paper' that propound that, 'We want to free the energies, talents and professional creativity of heads, governors and teachers and to create the conditions in which schools are freer to be innovative. The better schools given such freedom to innovate can lead the way in transforming secondary educational'

The White Paper in Britain is a good example of democratic education in the private schools. Through diversity, the government wants to encourage all schools to build a distinct ethos and center of excellence. Schools must develop the talents of each individual pupil to the full. There is therefore, a greater choice to both parents and students and to have different preferences. In Britain, the choice is not on merit of money to parents but to education quality. The government core values that must underline any educational reform can be set as the following three core principles; raising standards in education, enhancing opportunity for all and promoting the virtues of choice, diversity and innovation in education.

The reforms that have harnessed the private sector to improve education are the alternative funding. The difference with Zimbabwean education system, the private sector schools are not funded by the government unlike in Britain who give voucher /coupon or cheques to parents to spend with on education provider of their choice i.e., private school or public school for their children.

b. Sweden and Chile

The only two countries with University vouchers are Sweden and Chile. The Swedish voucher scheme is probably the most radical market reform in existence anywhere in the world, "The Swedish reforms occurred in 1992, when Municipalities were obliged to give 85% of the calculated average cost per student in the municipal schools to any school of parent choice for all students, not just targeted groups. Enrolment rules were also opened within the public sector, with money following the pupils into public sector schools in other municipalities. The figure of 85% was calculated so as to give equal funding to the independent schools", (Tooley, Dixon, Stranfield, 2003:45)

In Zimbabwe in particular, teachers are paid by the government but the students pay for their education while in Sweden, both private and public sector schools are distributed equally in the budget. More than that, as long as the schools fulfill certain requirements, any kind of school is eligible, from religious schools to schools run by for Profit Corporation. This is different from the situation in Denmark and the Netherlands, where private schools have had a long tradition of receiving public funding but only particular kinds or parents – controlled, not for profit schools are allowed to receive public funds. A rapid growth of independent schools has been experienced since the reforms were introduced.

Some municipalities estimate that private school's enrolment will grow to 50% in the next few years. In Colombia, a target voucher system was introduced in 1992, aimed at providing wider access to private education for poor students, inspired by the realization that they were a shortage of places offered by state secondary schools. The proposal allowed poor children to benefit from private school provision, moving out of the overcrowded public schools. The private schools taking part offer an educational service that had been estimated to be of comparable quality to that found in government schools and yet the typical cost of sending a pupil to private school via the voucher scheme, is two thirds of the per-pupil cost of sending him/her to a government school.

The fact is that the principle of support of private education is well established across mainland Europe. Public subsidy of private schools in the Netherlands ensuring freedom of parental choice in education has been in operation for almost 100 years. Although about 70% of children attend private schools, the majority of which are church schools with a total of 7% at non-religious private schools. All government and private grants schools are guaranteed the same financial support, hence the incentives, benefits of academic staff are attractive and high performance is guaranteed. Interestingly, although private schools are not allowed to charge top-up fees, they are allowed to receive contributions from parents to purchase teaching materials, fund extracurricular activities, employ additional staff or pay teachers a supplement to their regular salaries.

c. Denmark

In European Union countries all government and private grant aided schools are guaranteed the same financial support. Public subsidy of private schools in Denmark shares with the Netherlands the key features that there is constitutional right for parents to set up their own schools and receive state funding. All approved private schools are entitled to receive state subsidies covering about 80% of their operational expenditure on the basis of the number of pupils enrolled at an individual school in a given year. When a school determines its destiny, its performance is improved as they would be having resources at their disposal i.e., material to improve the facilities, money to supplement their staff and time management. "On top of these grants, parents pay a moderate fee, something long accepted in Denmark, as an important principle of family responsibility" (Stenhouse, 1975:144).

d. Germany

Rebore (1991:120) asserts that "Public subsidy of private schools that the private education is expanding at a remarkable rate because the leadership of the school determine high performance. Private education in German is significantly higher than in the United Kingdom. As such, private schools are allowed to charge their extra costs. They are also not required to follow the same time tables or curricula as public sector schools and also free to choose their textbooks" They are also free to promote religious or philosophical views and use teaching methods of their own choice. Moreover, private schools have complete freedom to hire and fire teaching staff hence having effective and efficient teaching staff. The leadership, which is participatory and democratic, has competent quality teachers and students for better performance and good results.

e. Hong Kong

Fee-paying schools are permitted to charge fees. To counteract the argument that the introduction of school fees will exclude children from low-income families, the government introduced a fee remission policy. "This is designed to channel a percentage of funds collected from fees into subsidized places to be poor. While for profit companies are allowed to operate schools, the majority of publicity funded schools in Hong Kong are owned and managed by churches, trust and private organizations" (Tooley et al, 2003:45).

f. United States of America

"Charter schools in USA are free from direct administrative government control and are under fewer regulatory constraints than state schools. They must however, meet the performance standards set by their charter. This freedom allows charter schools to have more control over their curriculum, hours of operations, the staff they employ, budget and internal organization and schedule" (Worths, 1990:37). This entails that private owned and run schools have high potential to excel because they are in control of the performance of the school than state-controlled schools. The leadership styles can determine the high or low performance, depending on who is on the leadership. The administration of the school calls for diligence, clear vision and goal achievement oriented.

"Education planning includes theory and practice, relevant research, consultation, policy formulating, decision making etc. and involvement of persons and bodies such as ministers, secretaries and directors of education, various advisory committees, institutions for educational research, academic etc." (Wincharuck, 1988).

g. Kenya

Basically, the public /state schools, the style of leadership and administration in Europe, Asia and America differ to some extent. "calculating the average rate of returns to higher education in Kenya under the full subsidy system in 1971 Fields shows that the private rate of return for form 6 education was around 17% in contrast with about 30% which was the corresponding figure for University education" (Dalta, 1984:32). The author concludes that the private rate of returns to education in Kenya were very high compared to rates earned in United Kingdom, the USA and some other countries. The rate of return in private schools is lower than the rate of return in public schools in that the fees in public schools is calculated with the benefits of the community mind.

The educational benefits and investments precipitate the private sector schools to have better standard of education compared to public sector schools.

Parents send their children to private schools in order to excel and get the best education and results while the public schools usually have poorer students who do not have enough finances and perform poorly academically. The importance of the school, as an agency of change has been underlined since independence by the leaders of modern African societies.

President Julius Nyerere in his academic paper wrote that education for self-reliance and he stressed that the education provided by Tanzania for students of Tanzania must encourage the growth of self-reliance and enhance the country's development.

Cost Benefit Analysis

Both private and public schools thrust in educating the citizens is to invest in the country, families and individuals for economic development. There is an obvious problem facing Policy formulators who want to reduce the financial costs of education to poor households. Any reduction, therefore, in household spending is not compensated for by an increase in public spending will other things being equal, reduce overall investment in education, with damaging implications for service provision and service quality. "Public investment in education is among the most cost-effective ways of reducing poverty, boosting economic growth and promoting basic human rights. In many countries, public spending is reduced by inefficiencies and inequitable spending patterns. Progress towards the goals of universal and free basic education, therefore, requires an enhanced role for publicity financed services" (Watkins, 2000:206).

Watkins continues to highlight that one of the consequences of under-investment by government has been a proliferation of private sector initiatives, some of which are supported by donors. "The inadequacies of public education systems have been driven to poor households into private systems. Ultimately, governments have the responsibility to carry out the public expenditure reforms needed to support free and compulsory primary education" (Watkins, 2000).

Sub-Saharan African spends a higher proportion of its GDP on education than any other developing region. The importance of economic growth to education financing is powerful in Africa not just in terms of comparisons with higher growth regions. "In 1970, Sudan was spending more per capita on education than Botswana in the public schools and private schools. Today, Botswana is spending four times as much, not because of an increased public expenditure ration but because of much faster growth. Even good performers in Sub-Saharan African have suffered the consequences of slow growth. Zimbabwe has one of the World's highest proportions of GDP allocated to education, but even so, real per capital investment remained static during the 1980's as a consequence of economic stagnation. If Zimbabwe had matched Thailand's rate of growth since 1990, real per capita spending levels would be almost double the current levels" (Watkins 1998:209).

Most of the developing countries that have achieved rapid growth and progress towards universal basic education from a weak starting point have spent 5-7 percent of GDP on education. In Sub-Saharan Africa, countries such as Chad, Mali, Tanzania and Zambia are spending less than 3 percent of GDP on education far too litter to meet basic education needs.

For much of the 19th century, private financing and philanthropy dominated the provision of education in the industrialized countries. Later on, in the twentieth century, as awareness of education increased, most government prioritized public provision, especially in basic education. Advocates of an enlarged role for the private sector are gaining a momentum. They indicate the potential private provision in extending choice, increasing accountability within the school system and reducing pressure on over-stretched budgets. In places of an unequivocal commitment to Universal public provision of good quality basic education, donors and governments are emphasizing the virtues of private –public partnership.

The private sector is becoming an increasingly important provider of education across much of the developing world. Private education providers range from community-run schools to schools run as a commercial business. Educating, the financing in private sector schools in some cases, makes the costs of supportably 'free' public education make private education a competitive opinion. The rate of children attending private schools rises with parental income, more than half the families in the lowest income societies were choosing private education for the children, in most African countries. Households surveys found that poor households cited that teacher's absenteeism in government schools as their main reason for choosing private schools.

Basically, leadership is required in every organization, company, school or in a family. The schools that we have in Zimbabwe need leadership that calls for development. To be a good and effective leader, it means you have to be able to use tools you are familiar with. "Leadership involves logistics, information, people and systems. It controls budgets, measures performance, monitor progress and initiatives corrective action" (Marshall, 1996:67).

In public schools, leadership style is usually authoritative because the policies and power is from central point's i.e., from superiors, district officers, permanent secretary, directors and deputy directors and from the Ministry of Education. In comparison with the private schools, leadership is mostly democratic, where they sit and discuss progress and development of the school.

Leadership is the art of getting things done. An effective leader trains and teaches the subordinates. Effective leadership means getting things done. Effective leadership means objectives are accomplished through people thus democratic leadership. Wincharuck, (1988:55) propounds that "Leadership is the art of combining ideas, people, things, time and energy to achieve predetermined objectives." One would concern with Wincharuck that leadership is in three ways; doing things to people; doing things for people and doing things with people.

Dr. Meyers on Manna Channel (Satelight dish) on the topic; Excellent leadership said that, "Managers deal with policies but leaders deal with people. Leaders have visions while managers have targets." To add on his concept, leadership involves the development and articulation of shared vision. In the private sector schools, there is usually a shared vision to progress compared to public schools where leadership is authoritative.

Goals and standards in any school must be jointly constructed and realistically accented by both the person and his/her supervisor. The reason for having objectives and goals for a school is to do a particular job. Performance standards help people develop their potentials. Standard facilities both do self-appraisal and review of one's performance with another person. A performance standard in a school is a measurement by which performance can be evaluated.

The Administration of The Schools in Private and Public Schools

Each school, both private and public has administration to run the school. Administration is a process whose aim is to achieve some specific goals or objectives in any given organization. Administration is a performance-oriented task. Administration is the management of daily activities and duties at a given institution. It is organization of programs in an organization. "Administration is the task of discovering and clarifying the goals and purpose of the field it serves and moving in a coherent, comprehensive manner towards their realization" (Lingren, 1998:23). One would concur with Lingren that administration is involving policy making as well as implanting those policies.

Both public and private schools should have short- and long-range planning in order to foster development in its administration. Planning is decided in advance as to what should be done, why it should be done, where it should be done, when and who should do it and how it should be done. If the administration of a school is poor, does not have a vision for its school, staff and students, it's calling for its collapse.

The administration of any school is the hope of its own destiny hence it should formulate its policies that tallies with its vision and objectives. In private education system, there is high quality education compared to public school. But sometimes, crude contrasts between 'low quality' private systems and 'high quality' private systems are misleading. In many countries, only the wealthy can afford good-quality private schools.

Private school of inferior quality are more affordable to the poor, but they do not offer the advantages often assumed for private education. Traditionally, the training of educational administrators has taken place in specialized institutes of Education and in the faculties of Education of various Universities. "The urgency attached to management training in education has led in recent years to the establishment of specialized institutions for this purpose. The two most developed of such institutions in English speaking Africa are the Kenya Education Staff Institution in Kenya and the Management Training for Education personnel Institutions in Tanzania" (Mbamba, 1992:13).

Staff Development in Schools

In some other African countries, the establishment of staff development institutes have been successful. In Zimbabwe Open University, was opened specially to cater for those who are already employed and would want to further their studies while at work. "There are many public administration institutes in Africa which include the administrative staff college of Nigeria, Zimbabwe Institute of Public Administration and Eastern and Southern Africa Management Institute which serves many countries in Africa." (Mbamba, 1992:13).

Training the staff for development is very fundamental as it improves confidence and quality when it comes to performance. In order to facilitate this process, well compiled, presented and properly constructed training material become imperative to the management development exercise.

Teacher Impact

Teacher motivation shows high medium impact and discriminates the excellent and very good schools.

The goals of the personnel function are basically the same in all school systems. It is to hire, retain, develop and motivate personnel in order to achieve the objectives of the school, to assist individual members of the staff to reach the highest possible levels of achievement is to maximize the career development of personnel.

The public schools do have specified elements of motivating the staff to perform high. Encouragements, appreciation and incentives are some of the major elements to motivate the staff in order to feel valuable and contribute significantly. When the school head recognize the value of person both as an individual and as a team member, when he commands a person's work, then one's work become easier and more rewarding.

"A staff development program centers around creating instructional learning situations. Learning is change in human capability, that can be retained and which is not simply ascribable to the process of growth." (Rebone 1991:164). The primary purpose of a staff development program is to increase the knowledge and skills of employees and thereby increase the potential of the school to attain its goals and objectives. There are three methods of development of staff that can be used.

Off-The-Job-Training

This includes various programs such as lectures, seminars, workshops, programmed instructions. The lecture method is best suited to conveying information such as procedures, methods and rules. In Zimbabwe the teaching staff are granted study-leave to further their studies in various universities/ colleges in their areas of specialization in order to enhance their professions. The staff development programs enhance high performance, integrity, effectiveness on job performance of schools both private and public schools. "The World Bank report on the quality of education in private schools and cities that the main incentives that attract young people to teaching in Liberia including payment of salaries on time, good housing, adequate instructional materials in classrooms and sufficient opportunities for development" (Lockheed and Verspoor, 1990:64).

"The Zimbabwe National Teacher Education Course (ZINTEC) is a well-known example of the combination of short periods of residential training with longer periods of distance training of teachers in the field. It was started in newly Independent Zimbabwe in 1981 in response to the need for a large increase teacher number to cope with requirements" (Avolas, 1991:42). Besides, better condition of service better benefits, salary increment, improved housing, staff development is one of the incentives to develop high performance and better result points in government schools i.e., public schools.

Education System in Zimbabwe

The government of Zimbabwe, the Ministry of Education, has the mandate to design and produce curriculum and syllabuses for both public and private schools. The design and control are centralized. What could be the reason for growth of privatization of schools in Zimbabwe. It is generally contended that there is a greater efficiency of the private sector schools. In the context of privatization, increased efficiency is not just a fiscal concept but it should be viewed as response to widespread dissatisfaction with government growth.

Many people in Zimbabwe, especially the education fraternity, share the belief that government has become synonymous with waste and inefficiency and that the public would be better served if government utilized more private companies to provide services. The central question raised is that "Public education has been a state-controlled monopoly for too long. Privatization would bring a greater range of choices to the public unmatched innovation to public education. Position two maintains that privatization and is unlikely to deliver the promised efficiencies increases in quality and that it represents a threat to the social and democratic goals of public education" (Nelson and Carlson, 1996:323).

Effective schools do not follow mechanical curricula. Effective teachers present lessons thoughtfully and reflectively, changing what they do in response to the ways in which students are learning. Successful schools are led by teachers who have control over resources, classroom time, instructional materials and teaching strategies and who make curriculum decisions. For schools to be effective, every teacher must share in the authority to make essential curricular decisions about how to teach and how to interact with students. There is now worldwide recognition of private enterprises as the key vehicle for improving the life of citizens while becoming more efficient with available funds and resources.

Schools are basic to the national interest and international competition. Zimbabwe's leadership depends on top-quality, well, educated people i.e., successful students from achievement driven schools. In Zimbabwe, the most important reason to involve private enterprise in schools is our children. Our primary resources deserve the best schools we can provide. "Well-run schools, where success is the motivating purpose, are appreciated by both parents and students. The faceless bureaucracy created for government-operated schools not only overwhelms local budgets, but it also does not meet the needs. Private enterprises could not survive with that approach, its success is linked to increasing efficiency and customer satisfaction" (Nelson, 1996:381).

Privatization will also increase accountability, making school staff responsible for mentoring performance standards for the benefit of the children. Accountability, a keystone of private enterprise, offers the means to clearly identify problems and to reward performance in schools. Private enterprise set specific goals and measures the performance of schools. The public schools in Zimbabwe, confirmed by researchers, have established a monopoly over taxpayer.

The public schools have been a monopoly for too long and they suffer the results of lack of competition. These schools have little reason to provide better service, increase their efficiency, require higher standards or eliminate layers of bureaucracy. The rate of return analysis is a form of cost benefit analysis that requires information on both the public and private costs of schooling as measured by lifetime earnings. The actual calculation compares the costs and benefits of a particular quality, type and level of education over time and finds the rate at which the present value of the benefit is equal to the present value of the costs.

If the rate of return of public investments in secondary education is 10 percent and recurrent rates are 5 percent then the public investments in basic education are better investments, on average than are savings. By the same token, if the public rate of return to higher education and savings are preferred to investments in higher education, on savings, is 5 percent then both investments in basic education and savings preferred to investments in higher education. "The purpose of these cost analysis is to help identify inefficiencies steaming from the way in which government allocates its resources and inefficiencies in the way resources are used" (Kemmer, 1994:22).

The researches in Zimbabwe show that better educated parents have demanded more for their children's education with successive generations of students being encouraged to match or exceed the educational levels of their parents attained. "The extent of differences between schools in their effectiveness became widely recognized during the 1980s as well as the need to do something about them central to the whole strategy is the ability to raise pupils' performances by securing year-on-year improvements in their effectiveness," (Hunter, 1998:3).

In the same vein, teachers are the school's greatest assets. They stand at the interface of the transmission of knowledge, skills and values.

Teachers will only be able to fulfill their educational purpose if they are both well prepared for the profession and able to maintain and improve their contributions to it, through career-long learning. The private schools develop the welfare of their teachers as compared to public schools. Support for the well-being and professional development is therefore, integral and essential part of efforts to raise standards of teaching, learning and achievement. The research in Zimbabwe reveals that most of the teachers put their own efforts to develop their careers and professions than the institutions they are serving.

Continuing career long professional development is necessary for all teachers in order to keep pace with technical and development and renew their own knowledge, skills and visions for good teaching. Successful development in education is dependent upon successful teacher development. Planning and supporting career long development is the joint responsibility of teachers, schools and government. To have competent, skilled, result oriented and high-performance teachers, there is a need to have professional development and central in maintaining and enhancing the quality of teachers and the leadership roles of principals. "Many teachers continue to work in overcrowded classrooms with both students and teachers feeling overwhelmed, discouraged and often disgusted. A survey of the opinions of 599 students and 200 teachers in public schools found out that overcrowding was having significantly negative effects on instruction and learning in the system," (Day, 1999:16).

The researches that have been done do not compare the effectiveness, efficiency and high performance of schools both in the private and public schools and also in-terms of leadership. Mugodzwa, (1999:7) asserts that "Schools in Zimbabwe reveal considerable variations, private schools differ in many ways from government schools which in turn differ significantly from rural secondary schools and mission schools." He continues to say that high fee-paying schools have excellent facilities and because of the prohibitively high fees they charge, cater for the wealthier classes in the society. Government schools are cheaper and characterized by inadequate facilities and high enrolment, hence performance for both teachers and students is low because of lack of adequate textbooks, furniture, classroom material in the form of stationery crowdedness and some educational facilities, because of these factors they produce poor results.

The poor 'O' Level results by rural day schools has become a matter of great national concern. Below is a list of headlines from the local media in Zimbabwe.

"What are the causes of the high rate of failure in rural schools" (Teacher in Zimbabwe; 1994:21). The newspaper was analyzing the rate of failure of 'O' Level examination of which 95% are government and council schools.

"Zimbabwe's education system is tribulation for the poor" (Herald, February 1991:1). It means everybody is concerned about the rate of failures of our students because of lack of better facilities, unmotivated teachers, inadequate textbooks, low benefits and not attractive incentives to the staff. In privately owned schools, the pass rate in 1992 averaged 90% (Ministry of Education, 1992). "The same trend has not changed to date as evidenced by the 1998 'O' Level results in which well-funded schools like St Ignatius College scored a 100% pass rate, while most of the schools performed badly" (Zimbabwe Examination Council, 1999:6). This is clear evidence that the public schools are not only underperforming but are disadvantaged in the education system.

The leadership in the public schools, therefore must put more effort in providing quality education through improved infrastructure development, teaching materials, the quality of instructing and reducing the proportion of untrained teachers. "A school with better teaching and learning facilities tends to attract better qualified teachers." (Nyawaranda, 1993:13).

In Zimbabwean education, educational reform is a local process. The school is the center of change, not the Ministry or district administration. For the schools to improve the quality of their programs effectively, they need to play an active and creative role. Good materials and facilities are necessary. Teacher's mastery is crucial for impact on students and can best be developed through a systematic local learning process that includes in-service training and supervision and coaching in a collegial atmosphere. Commitment is essential at all levels. Sustained efforts and maintenance of needed support structures are crucial at the central level. Parents and community participation contribute to success. Parents and community participation lead to commitment and have an effect on the outcome.

Summary of The Chapter

As a matter of fact, researches, in parts of the world, in Britain, Hong Kong, USA and Denmark patterning private compared to public schools in terms of leadership vary according to their educational systems. In Britain, for example, they have core principles of values the education system aims to achieve i.e., equality, opportunity for all, autonomy and diversity. The government requires and encourages all schools to build a distinct ethos and center for excellence. In Hong Kong, publicly funded schools are permitted to charge fees. The majority of publicly funded schools in Hong Kong are owned by churches. In USA Charter schools are free from direct administrative government control. In Denmark, independent schools operate at a per capita per pupil cost. The analysis of these educational systems in Europe and America enables the leadership to realize as they manage their schools without government control, as it were.

In Africa, the researches show that there are private schools, which are owned, by missions, companies, organizations and individual who operate autonomously but the curriculum and syllabus are designed and implemented by the governments. The Tanzania, Zambia and to some extent, Sub-Saharan Africa have private schools managed by the owners although examination boards and the ministries of education take the big chunk. Public sector schools suffer because of lack of facilities, stationery, textbooks, libraries, classrooms, furniture, and infrastructures etc., hence poor results and under performance.

In Zimbabwe educational system, the private schools are owned and controlled by churches, organizations, companies, individuals. The leadership in schools in pre-independence was pro-white minority and white community benefited in the education arena. In post-independence, there was wave of change in education system, which was instituted by ZANU-PF which called for education for all, regardless of creed, color, race, rich or poor, young and old. Subsequently, public schools expanded hence resources dropped thus affected effective performance, efficiency, effectiveness and competence. The curriculum and syllabuses were centralized.

The leadership styles in schools are basically, in three folds i.e., autocratic leadership, authoritative leadership and democratic leadership. In private schools most of the time, there is democratic or participatory leadership. The school administration calls everyone to participate although some privately owned schools are autocratic in nature because of their leadership. The administration of any school is the only hope for excellence and high performance. Public schools should have staff development plan to enhance better performance.

The next chapter will now describe and explain the research methodology used in this study. It will also explain the research design, sample and data collection procedures

CHAPTER THREE
Research Methodology

Introduction

In this chapter, the methodology used to carry out the research is explained. The research design is described and justified. The data collection methods and procedures together with instruments used to collect and how they were administered are all explained. The chapter will conclude by describing the methods used to analyze the data.

Research Design

The study followed the survey research design. The survey design was appropriate for the study because as Isaac and Michael (1984:128) puts it. Surveys are a means of gathering information that describes the frequencies of attitudes, opinions and views from a target population. This study seeks to establish the performance of private and public sector schools and the leadership styles in Zimbabwean Education. These will help in making evaluative conclusions on the performance of schools and the leadership styles and administration.

The survey design was used because it allows for use of a sample rather than the entire schools in Zimbabwe. It was not possible to include every school in Harare Metropolitan city because they are too many. A representative sample was selected and the results were generalized into the entire population. This is supported by Macmillan and Schumacher (1993:36) who explained that: "Usually the survey is designed such that information about a large number of people (population can be inferred from the responses obtained from a smaller group of subjects (sample)

Data Collection Methods

The data for the study were collected by means of questionnaires and interviews. Questionnaires provided data for the quantitative aspects of the study such as number of staff and students who had similar views and issues raised. The other sample provided data for the qualitative aspects such as the underlying reasons for the views made. They also created a forum for following up responses made in the questionnaires. The honesty accuracy and truthfulness of the staff and students' responses in questionnaires and interviews could then be assessed in order to come up with judgement on the performance and leadership styles in both private and public schools in Zimbabwe.

Population and Sample Population

According to Pilot and Hungler (1987:32) a population in research refers to "The entire set of individuals or objects, having a common character and to whom a research study would be applicable" The population for this study is all the staff and students at Hatfield High School and Phoenix College. There are 560 students and 27 teachers at Hatfield High School in 2007. There are 618 students and 23 teachers at Phoenix College in 2007.

The Sample and Sampling Procedure

Manelle (1990:42) stated that "A sample is drawn from a target population and it is representative if it accurately reflects the distribution of relevant variables in the target population. In this study a sample had to be drawn from both the students and staff population. The table below summaries the categories of students and staff who made up the sample.

Table 3.1. Composition of the sample used in the study

School	Number of staff	Number of students	Totals
Phoenix College	21	60	81
Hatfield High School	25	72	97
Grand Total	**46**	**132**	**178**

As reflected on the table, a total of 178 students and staff made up the sample. Students refer to forms one to six who were sampled. Staff refers to both teaching staff and non-teaching staff at these two respective schools. Hatfield High School is a public sector school and Phoenix College is a private sector school under the government.

In each case random sampling procedures were used. Twenty-one (21) staff was sampled at Phoenix College and twenty-five staff (25) was sampled at Hatfield High School. Sixty (60) students were sampled in Phoenix College and seventy-two (72) students were sampled at Hatfield School. This method approximates the Lottery method of random sampling described by Leedy (1980:112) in this way, "... the population is arranged sequentially and assigned a numerical identification. Corresponding numbers are marked on separate tabs and put in a revolving drum. Tabs bearing numbers are selected... without the selector seeing the poor."

Research Instruments

The instruments used to collect data for this study were questionnaires and interviews.

Questionnaires

A total of 178 questionnaires were filled in and returned by the respondents.

Students answered and returned 132 questionnaires whilst the staff filled and returned 46.

Questionnaires were useful for a study like this because as Nachmias and Nachmias (1989:83) propounded that they are characterized by anonymity. This was necessary and fundamental as the performance, leadership and administration of schools in public schools have been classified as failures of producing the best results nationwide.

The fact that the students and staff took the questionnaires home overnight to fill them reduced what Borg and Gall (1983:59) called "biasing errors" These arise from the influence of the researcher on the respondents. These influences were minimized because the respondents filled in the questionnaires in the absence of the researcher.

The questionnaires also gave the opportunity for the respondents to make considerable answers and to consult their personal comments if this became necessary. This was possible because they had 48 hours to work on the questionnaires.

However, limitations were experienced in using the questionnaires. There was no opportunity for probing by the researcher. Probing was necessary, especially where the responses given were ambiguous, unclear and controversial. "The answers given in a questionnaire have to be accepted as final as there is no opportunity to probe beyond the given answers" (Cohen and Manion,1997:241). Another problem was that after the first batch was dispatched, the response rate was not hundred percent. This increased the cost of the research as travels to collect more questionnaires doubled.

Interviews

These are the selected persons among the staff and the students by the researcher as sample. These interviews were helpful in that they helped to clear some of the controversial responses made in the questionnaires. These interviews provided a forum for the researcher to follow up on certain items so that the gaps in information are filled. The researcher interacted with the staff and students. A major setback about interviews which the researcher had to guard against was the possibility of influencing the interviewees in the way the researcher perceived. This was controlled by careful questioning and limiting comments by the researcher. The researcher asked critical questions perceived by the interviewees as fundamental in public and private leadership and administration. As a result, the data required was collected.

Data Collection Procedures

The following procedures were followed in preparing the instruments and collecting data.

Pre-Testing the Questionnaires

The questionnaire was pre-tested on 10 students and 8 staff of Phoenix College. They were asked to answer it and make comments on any questions that were unclear or could not be answered easily. The questions, which both the staff and students were unclear and uncomfortable with, were removed from the questionnaires. These included those that were vague to them and those they felt required information that was too personal. Finally, 25 questions items questionnaire was developed and administered.

Administration of The Questionnaires

The researcher personally administered the questionnaires. The researcher asked for permission from the school authority to distribute the questionnaires during break time. They were asked to bring the questionnaires after 48 hours to give them adequate time to answer honestly, accurately and truthfully. They requested to slot the answered questionnaires under an agreed door at each school, i.e., to senior teachers' office, to maintain anonymity. This was done and average 75% return rate was achieved. Further sampling and administration of questionnaires was done until the required numbers were obtained.

Data from Phoenix College and Hatfield High School

The students and staff from each school were sampled and interviewed. The data collected reflected genuineness and honesty.

Data Analysis Plan

All the data obtained from questionnaires was tallied and converted to percentages wherever this was possible. Responses from the staff were kept separate from students in order to allow comparison and variance. Tables were then developed, each number with a number and heading showing the varying responses and the percentage of respondents who made them. Data obtained from interviews were incorporated into the relevant sections of the questionnaires. These put more substance to the responses made in the questionnaire, making it easier for the researcher to make interpretations and conclusions.

Summary

Basically, this chapter has described and explained the research methodology. Details of the research design, sample and data collection procedures were elucidated. The next chapter i.e., chapter four, the data will be presented followed by a discussion in which the data are interpreted. Answers to the research questions will be made in that chapter.

CHAPTER FOUR

Data Presentation, Analysis and Intepretation

Introduction

In this chapter the data collected by means of questionnaires and interviews is presented, described, analyzed and discussed.

The first section shall present all the data collected in tables, bar graphs and pie charts. In the second section, the data is analyzed to bring out relations, patterns and themes. In the third and final segment, a discussion is carried out to show how the data answers the research questions and how compares with the findings in the literature review. The information collected from the interviews shall be used during the interpretation to add meaning to the data collected using questionnaires.

Data Presentation and Description

The data is presented in two major dimensions. The perceptions of the students and staff in the private schools compared with those in the public sectors referred to as Government schools. Totals of 127 and 51 students and teachers respectively provided the data which leads to a total of 178 respondents from both Government and private schools. Students and staff perceptions from both private and government schools provided the data.

Table 4.1. Distribution of Respondents by school

	Private School (N=81)		Government schools (N=97)	
Respondents	No.	%	No.	%
Students	60	74	67	69
Staff	21	26	30	31
Total	**81**	**100**	**97**	**100**

The table shows that more students from the private school provided the data, that is 74% whilst students from Government schools were 69%. Staff from the government school were 31% while those from private school were 26%. More students from a private school provided the data than those from a government school by a difference of 5% while more staff from the government school provided than those from a private school by a difference of 5% as well.

Table 4.2. Distribution of students' respondents by school

	Private School (N=81)		Government schools (N=97)	
Age in years	No.	%	No.	%
13 & below	10	17	19	28
14-16	18	30	30	45
20-22	4	8	3	4
23-25	5	8	0	0
Totals	**60**	**100**	**67**	**100**

The table shows that the majority of students at Phoenix College are between the ages of 17-19 years with 37% while at Hatfield High School 5%. No student from Hatfield High School has 23-25 years while at Phoenix College there are (5) which is 8%. Students below 13 years are more Hatfield High School, that is 28% while at Phoenix College there are 17%.

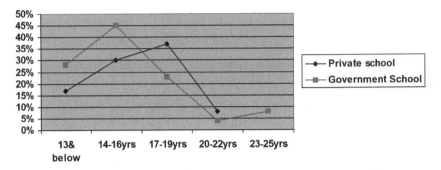

Fig 4.1. A comparison of age distribution of students between private and government

This figure shows that 17 of the private school students were aged 13 years and below whilst in the Government school these were 28%. In the private school 30% were aged 14-16 years whilst in the Government school these were 45%. In the Government school 23% were aged 17-19 years while those in the private school were 37%. 4% of the Government school was aged 4% while those in the private school were 8%. No one was aged 23-25 years in the Government school while in the Private school was 8%.

Table 4.3. Percentage of pass rates at Phoenix College and
Hatfield High School for 'O' and 'A' Levels

	PASS RATES IN PERCENTAGES %			
	Phoenix College		Hatfield High School	
Years	'o' level	'A' Level	'O' Level	'A' Level
2004	47.2	71.3	-	-
2005	68	60	28	72
2006	57.3	66	24	68

The table above shows that for the year 2004 Phoenix College had 47, 2% and 71,3% for 'O' and 'A' levels respectively. For the year 2005 Phoenix College had 68% and 60% for 'O' and 'A' Level respectively for that same year. In 2006 Phoenix College had 57.3% for 'O' Level while Hatfield High School had 24% for that same level. In that same year Phoenix College had 66% for 'A' Level and Hatfield High School had 68% for that same year.

From the results, the pass rate for Phoenix College for 'O' Level is generally higher than that of Hatfield High School. While at 'A' Level the pass rates are almost the same but slightly higher at Hatfield High School.

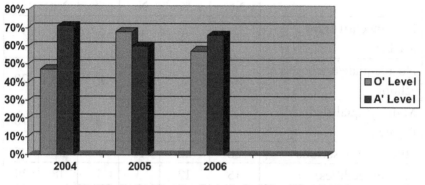

Fig 4.2. Pass rates of Phoenix College for 'O' and 'A' Levels

This graph indicates that the pass rates for 'A Level are generally higher than those of 'O' Level. For 'A' Level the highest pass rate was in 2004 with 71.3% while the highest pass rate for 'O' Level was in 2005 with 68%. For the three consecutive years all the percentages for 'A' level are above 50% while for A' Level there is 47.2% for the year 2004.

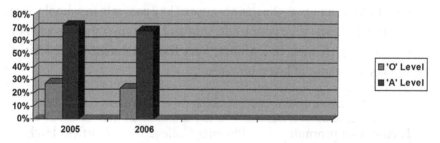

Fig 4.3. Pass rate of Hatfield High School for 'O' Level and 'A' Level

The graph shows that in 2005 the pass rate was 28% and 72% for 'O' and 'A' level respectively. For the year 2006 the pass rate was 24% and 68% for 'O' and 'A' level are all below 50% while those for A' Level are all above 50%

Table 4.4. Responses on the causes of low pass rate in a school

Cause of Low pass rate	Frequency of responses					
	Students (N=127)		Staff (N=46)		Total	
	No.	%	No	%	No	
Poor incentives for teachers	10	7	16	35	26	42
No adequate textbooks at school	6	5	7	15	13	20
Many unqualified teachers	7	6	2	4	9	10
Students not serious	28	22	11	23	39	45
Lack of facilities	15	12	3	7	18	19
Poor leadership &administration	37	29	4	9	41	38
Lack of efficiency of staff and students	24	19	3	7	27	26
Total	127	100	46	100	173	200

The table above shows that most teachers i.e. (35%) indicated poor incentives for teachers as the major cause of low pass rate in school while most students (29%) gave poor leadership and administration as a major cause for low pass rates in a school. Very few students (5) gave lack of textbooks as a cause of low pass rates.

Table 4.5. Factors that promote high pass rate in a school

Factors that promote high pass rates	Phoenix College (N=81)		Hatfield High (N=97)	
	No	%	No	%
Committed Teachers	16	20	25	26
Hardworking students	40	49	45	46
Availability of textbooks	25	31	27	28
Total	81	100	97	100

This tables shows that 20% of the respondents at Phoenix believe that the teachers commitment contributes to the high pass rates while those at Hatfield High School were 26%. Those that believe that the student's hardworking matters were 49% and 46% for Phoenix College and Hatfield High School respectively. For availability of textbooks were 31% and 28% for Phoenix College and Hatfield High School respectively.

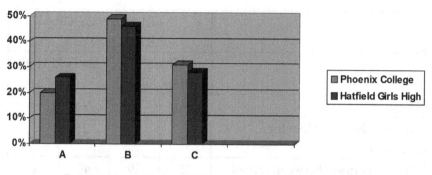

Fig 4.4. Factors that promotes high pass rates of students at a school

The graph above shows most respondents from both Phoenix College and Hatfield High School gave hardworking students as the most factor that promote high pass rate i.e., 49% and 46% for Phoenix College and Hatfield High School respectively for committed teachers its was 20% and 25% for Phoenix College and Hatfield High School respectively. Availability of text books had 31% for Phoenix College and 28% for Hatfield High School.

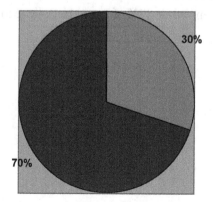

Fig 4.5. Perceptions of respondents on whether all schools should be under the Government (N=178)

The figure above shows that only (53) 20% of the respondents think that not all schools are to be Government school while those that think that all schools should be government schools were 125 (70%). Reasons as to why all schools should be government schools were investigated and they are given on Table 4.6 below.

Table 4.6. Reasons why all schools should be Government school

	FREQUENCY OF RESPONSES %			
	Phoenix College (N=81)		Hatfield High (N=97)	
Reason	'No	%	No	%
Affordable school fees for everyone	52	64	23	24
No competition between school	15	19	40	41
Creates sense of unity among Zimbabweans citizens	14	17	34	35
Total	81	100	97	100

Most respondents at Phoenix College (64%) gave the reason that school fees will be available for everyone while on that same reason for Hatfield High School it was 25%. No competition between schools was 19% and 41% for Phoenix College and Hatfield High School respectively. 35% of Hatfield High School respondents think that it will create a sense of Unity among Zimbabwean Citizens while 17% of Phoenix College for that same reason.

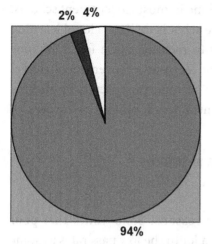

2% 4%

■ Yes
■ No
□ Not Sure

94%

Fig 4.6. Percentages of respondents on whether leadership and administration
do contribute to the performance of both students and staff in schools

Figure 4.6 shows that the majority of respondents think that leadership and administration do contribute to the pass rate of a school that is 167 (95%). Only (4) 2% think that it does not contribute while (7) 4% were not sure.

Data Analysis

Interviews were held for both staff and teachers from both schools, that is Phoenix College and Hatfield High School. The data that follows was obtained from the interviews. A total of 10 respondents were interviewed, five from each school, that is 3 and 2 staffs and students respectively.

Responses from students on which school they prefer (private to government)

Out of the four students from both schools 3 of them responded that they would prefer a private school than a Government school. Their reasons for this response were investigated and they gave the following reasons: Private schools offer a variety of sporting activities like swimming, golf and many others which are not done in most Government schools. Another reason was that most private schools do have a lot of learning resources like textbooks, computers to mention but a few. Only one student sad that she would prefer to learn at a Government school giving the reasons that private schools promote promiscuity by offering a variety of entertainments and too much freedoms for the learners.

Responses from staff on the causes of failure rates in Government schools

On this question staff gave varying reasons. Some think that poor incentives for teachers do contribute a lot to the low pass rates as some teachers will spend time doing their own business trying to make ends meet instead of doing remedial work for students. Some think that the low pass rate is caused by teachers who teach subjects they do not specialize in while others think that lack of textbooks and other teaching resources leads to low pass rates. Others think that pupils these days are now mischievous due to the issue of children's rights which they misuse by being arrogant and lack of respect for teachers, this will lead to low pass rates.

Responses on whether all schools should be run by the Government

This interview questions were focused on the staff who gave a variety of perceptions. Most of them think that (94%) they should run by the Government as this will remove the spirit of superiority and inferiority complex thus creating a sense of unity among Zimbabwean citizens. Some think that the Government offers an affordable school fees so it will foster and allow many people to afford school fees. Some think that teachers will stay longer at a school as they will be no competition around them in terms of payments and incentives thereby improving pass rates in school.

Demographic features of student's respondents from both private and Government schools

Figure 4.1 shows that for Government schools there are more students who are 16 years old and below than in the private school. A point to note is that as the years increases, the percentage also increases in the private school, that is for those who are above 17 years they were more than in the Government school. This is probably due to the fact that most repeaters do go to private schools as it is easier to get places to enroll than in the Government schools. Private schools are not strict in terms of their selection than in Government schools. However, the sample lies in the ages of 13-25 years.

Data Discussion

The study has established that most students prefer to learn at a private school because they think that Government schools are inferior to private schools. Most teachers think that the Government does not provide incentives for teachers and as a result, they will seek greener pastures like in the private schools.

This study has also established that in order to improve pass rates, the students themselves should be serious and hardworking. This was then seen as the major factor. Other factors were that there should be good leadership like in the supervision of both staff and students.

The study also found that for both schools, that is private and government schools the pass rates for 'A' level is far much higher than that of 'O' Level. This is probably due to the fact that students at 'A' level are a bit mature than 'O' level students such that they are aware of the importance of education. This could also be to the fact that most learners for 'A' level have higher 1. Q's as they would have passed the ordinary level, so they tend to pass more unlike at 'O' level where there is a mixture of slow and fast learners.

It was also interesting to note that the pass rate in the private school in the case Phoenix College were generally higher than in the Government school in this case, Hatfield High School that is for both 'O' and 'A' levels. This could be probably to the fact that the private schools do offer many resources such as textbooks, computers etc. than the Government schools.

The study also established that there are more mature students in terms of ages in the private school than in the Government schools to an extent that in private school they are some who are 23-25 years while there is no one with those years in a Government school. So, there are younger students at private schools than in Government schools.

Summary of the Chapter

This chapter has presented the data, made a description and analysis of it and ended with a discussion. The data has shown that most students will prefer to learn at private school for various reasons and also teachers would prefer private schools than Government schools as they provide incentives for teachers. Most students learn that Government schools are inferior to private schools, however, some think that students at private schools have too many freedoms thereby lacking discipline. Despite this perception, the pass rate in the private school is higher than in the Government schools.

The next chapter summarizes the whole book, draws conclusions and supplies recommendations for resolving different problems in both private and public schools.

CHAPTER FIVE

Summary, Conclusion and Recommendations

Introduction

This chapter summarizes the research study. It draws conclusions and recommendations for their future action. The summary includes highlights such as the research problem that was investigated, the purposes of the study and the major findings made. It synthesizes the four chapters.

Summary

This research study is intended to establish the reasons the public sector schools record low performance and poor pass rate and has poor leadership compared to private sector schools which is perceived and regarded as having higher performance and good pass rates and at the same time regarded as more efficient, competent and having effective leadership and administration. The two leadership of the two sector schools and the performance of the school was examined and determined if the assumptions were justified. The aim of the study was to establish facts and to determine the extent to which performance and leadership of the private and public government schools have affected the education system in Zimbabwe. This was to deduce whether both students and staff have adopted a new paradigm of thinking to change the performance for the better so that Zimbabwe will remain the envy and at the top of sub-Saharan Africa, as an educational giant in education fraternity.

The research design followed the survey design. There were five major findings made by this study. The first was related to lack of resources in a school especially the public schools (textbooks, furniture, science laboratories, facilities and infrastructure). It was established that whilst the two types of schools, the private and the public schools, followed the same education curriculum of the Ministry of Education. The students in the public schools highlighted lack of teaching resources as one of the major contributory factors in low performance and poor pass rates. Although it was also mentioned in the private sector schools, but it was at minimum level.

The second findings relate to inefficient, incompetent and non-visionary leadership and administration of the schools especially in the public schools. Respondents indicated that the leadership and administration of the schools contribute on poor pass rates and low performance, particularly in public schools compared to private sector schools. The leadership and administration were also recorded as a major contributory factor on school's failure to perform to the expected standard because it plans, implement and drives the schools to the desired position.

The third finding is that there is lack of adequate incentives, benefits and allowances to motivate the staff. The teachers and no academic staff in public school are demotivated, as there are no added allowances or benefits to boost their desires to work to their expected capacities. In private schools the staff are given extra benefits and other incentives to cater for their various needs. That alone increases their desires and willingness to work hard. In public schools, the staff's benefits and allowances are considered collectively and after their salaries have been eroded by hyperinflation what they get is what they give in terms of service hence low performance and poor pass rates are recorded.

The fourth finding is about both the students and teachers who are not merely committed and not serious about their work. The respondents indicated in some schools, both public and private sector schools that some teachers do not attend and teach their classes in regular intervals.

In the same vein, some students also are not serious and committed to their studies. They realize when it is too late that they were supposed to work harder in their studies in order to contribute to the good pass rates of their schools and for their future carriers. Others are naturally, incompetent, inefficient and lacking discipline, and some it is because of their own making.

The fifth and the final finding is about the government's interventions in education sector which does not warrant progress and successes. Most of the respondents, indicated that in the public schools, they are many strings attached to performances and pass rates to the Ministry of Education. For example, they control and determine school fees, they can improve the standard of test scores and they are responsible to improve school facilities such as laboratories and classrooms, including the incentives for the teaching stuff. In the private schools, they determine their own budgets to improve the facilities, can determine the incentives to give to their staff to motivate them and also to plan for staff development. The respondents indicated that if the government, the Ministry of Education, reduced or minimized their control on private sector schools, it would improve high performance and increase high pass rates in the private schools. Others contended that to privatize all education in Zimbabwe will be the best move to improve and it may enhance high performance in schools.

Research conclusions

The research draws the following conclusions. The first one is that although there is lack of resources in education systems especially, the public / government schools i.e., textbooks, facilities, infrastructure, furniture, science laboratory, and other resources to improve the running of the public schools they is still have great potential to thrive and turn around the public sector to be any of many students and parents to send their children. To have an effective and efficient school, it calls for the teachers, the stuff and the students to pull together and to utilize the available resources to achieve targeted goals. The public schools have great potential to exceed the expectations and be number one in standard scores if they prioritize and implement necessary changes to be successful. By the same token, the private schools can utilize the resources they accrue as they are not monitored by the government and have higher standard scores for their students. Although the private and public differ to some extent, especially on the delivery system, both sectors must plan and aim for higher performance from both the students and the staff.

- The second conclusion is that the leadership and the administration of any given school should deliver the educational services for the benefits of the students and their parents who cater for their children. It is an investment to both the students and the society at large. The high performance of a school does not bring glory to the school or to the country only but it improves the lives of the citizens who are able to determine their bright future. It is therefore imperative to foster high performance and pass rates and counting the costs in both sectors. It can therefore be further concluded that the leadership and administration of each school has a lot to do in order to bring the school to the high standard.
- The third conclusion is that both private and public / government schools are solely responsible to create conducive educational environment to both the staff and students to motivate them by providing attractive incentives, benefits, allowances, good accommodation, loans, facilities and good condition for learning and for working.
- The fourth conclusion is that teachers and students are to be encouraged to be serious about their work. Most of the time, students have questions that are not addressed. The teachers need better working conditions, incentives and benefits for them to work happily and to be committed.

As a whole, the two sector schools, i.e., private and public sector schools do have some differences. The surveys clearly indicated that Phoenix College, a private school had a high-test score and higher performance than Hatfield Girls High School, a public sector school. The perception of people to contend that private schools are better than public schools was justified although there are no major significance differences as such. The private sector schools have better facilities, sports, infrastructure, mostly of them with competent and efficient leadership and administration because they measure performance unlike most of public sector schools. Some of the private sector schools do not record successes as expected. The perception that Zimbabwean education is to be privatized is not acceptable to the government of Zimbabwe. However, both the staff and the students, from public and private sector schools indicated that, that could be another alternative to test the idea and that it may have the lasting solution to the education sector.

Recommendations

- This research study makes major recommendations to the Ministry of Education in Zimbabwe both private and public schools educate Zimbabwean citizens and the government must invest to both sectors.
- The leadership and administration of schools should be given liberty to plan, budget and implement both the government policies and private schools' policies independently.
- The government should not control the school's fees in private schools but let each school develop their own school fees, structure, salaries, benefits, allowances and other incentives for the staff of schools.
- The views of both the students and staff gathered in the interviews were that for public schools to improve their performance and pass rates, there is need to change the educational policies to suit the global standards.
- Students strongly felt that lack of educational resources hampered high performance and high pass rates hence the need to decentralize the whole educational system. This is a reasonable new particularly as this study has shown that at the two sector schools (Phoenix College and Hatfield High School), education is not done in isolation but together with other fundamental issues that affect people such as leadership, salaries, education resources, human rights education, social

benefits and condition of services. Staff development must be regarded as a priority to enhance better results.

- To school administration, especially in the public government schools, there is need to commit themselves into bringing their schools to the best level of educational excellence through staff development, creating better incentives for their staff and to motivate their students. The school should not look up to the government for funds but should engage into income generating projects for both student's and staff's welfare. Other resources such as television, video machines and international facilities are also necessary to put any school on the world map.

- To students firstly, the research recommended that students be disciplined, know their purpose in school and follow their visions and aspirations in life and to be serious with their studies. Secondly, students should concentrate on the subjects that they are passionate about and they good at. Thirdly, the students should develop a reading culture even during the holidays. Fourthly, the students should avoid to be derailed from their education focus by pleasures and involving themselves in unnecessary behaviors.

- To the Ministry of Education, especially the policy makers, the education curriculum should include lifesaving educational programs such moral education that instills moral behavior and impart moral values. By the same token the Ministry Education should limit the control of fees to private schools and public schools. The administration and leadership should be left to run and control their institutions fully to enhance high performance and high pass rates.

- Finally, the research study recommends three lines along with future research in comparison of private schools and public schools. One line of examination of the causes of under-performance in public sector is the caliber of administration and leadership in the Ministry of Education policy makers. The qualifications of the policy makers in the ministry of education should be examined. The second line of examination is the relevance of education in Zimbabwe as the colonial systems had its aims and objectives to achieve hence, they created a white color job education as their citizens who fill the managerial positions in the country. Therefore, there is need for policy makers to evaluate the education, which is offered in order to be relevant and cater for the economic changes and global inputs.

- A third dimension of research is to examine the behavioral modification models that would be practical and applicable to school student and staff. Appropriate behavior modification models should be now be put into place in schools so that with the information that students they have can be empowered to adopt high performance attitudes.

A very fundamental question of every parent lingers as they contemplate on where to send their children, to either a public school or a private school. They evaluate and access whether to send their children to public or private schools to best prepare them for the future? What are the cost benefits do public or private schools offer their children as the best investment? Which style of education are congruent with our family values? Which school is cost effective for my children? These are practical and real questions that the parents face when they are deciding for their children's future schools to attend. The parents have to assess and evaluate the benefits of either a private or public school if they are worth the costs. Some of the ethical decisions for the children is coined in the fact that range from personal to family values such as culture and faith.

At the end of the day, parents have to choose schools that will be the best for their children in terms of faith, culture that will bring the cost-effective outcome, with the best quality of education!! The best environment for their children will be the best choice. The other factor that helps parents in choosing the best schools for their children is the test scores history, the size of the classes, and the student and teacher ratio which plays a pivotal role. "The difference between the public and private school class size, and the student-to-teacher ratios, is considerable. In public schools, the average class size is 25 kids, compared to 19 kids per class in private schools according to NCES. Correspondingly, private schools have a better student-to-teacher ratio of 12.2 students, compared to 16.1 students per class." This is in the American context.

However, the study reveals that many gaps still exist so it is recommended that there be further research in the development of valid and reliable instruments to measure teacher effectiveness and student's competence.

APPENDIX I

Questionnaire for Staff and Students

This questionnaire is designed to collect data on the perceptions of students and staff in two schools, private and public in Harare on performance, leadership and administration. The data is for the research to be submitted to the Faculty of Education, Zimbabwe Open University, in partial fulfillment of the requirements for a Master's Degree in Education Administration, Planning and Policy Studies.

As a student and staff of Phoenix College and Hatfield Girls High School, your views will be highly appreciated and valued in this assessment and evaluation in order to improve education system in our schools.

Kindly supply your honest views and observations to the questions given. Your name is not necessary and you will remain anonymous but we only need your responses shall be kept in strict confidence and used for this only.

Kindly tick in the appropriate box or write in the spaces provided

1. I am ☐ Male ☐ Female
2. My age is
   ☐ 20 years and below
   ☐ 21 to 25 years
   ☐ 26 to 35 years
   ☐ 36 to 40 years
   ☐ 41 to 60 years

3. I am doing
   - ☐ Form three
   - ☐ Form four
   - ☐ Lower six
   - ☐ Upper six
   - ☐ Staff

4. In my school
   (Tick as many as are applicable)
   - ☐ Results/performance is high
   - ☐ Results/performance is low
     Leadership/Administration is good ☐   Poor ☐
     Facilities are conducive ☐   Not ☐
     Other ways: 1. ....
                   2. ....

5. Teachers are well qualified: (Tick)
   - ☐ Yes
   - ☐ No
   - ☐ Do not know

6. Teachers teach relevant subjects (Tick)
   - ☐ Yes
   - ☐ No
   - ☐ Most of them are
   - ☐ Do not know

7. How can education system in your school be improved? (Tick as many as are applicable)
   - ☐ By giving teachers better condition of service
   - ☐ By giving students better and conducive environment for learning
   - ☐ Increase school fees to by textbooks and furniture
   - ☐ Reduce intake

8. Which school do prefer to learn, private school or public/ government school?
   ☐ In private school but in urban
   ☐ In public school but in rural
   ☐ In council school
   ☐ In private school but rural
   ☐ In public school but in rural
   Other view: 1. ....
                  2. ....

9. In my opinion the factors that reduce pass rate in a school
   Are: (Tick where appropriate)
   ☐ Curriculum which is not relevant
   ☐ Teachers who are not serious
   ☐ No adequate textbook
   ☐ Students playful, not serious
   ☐ Lack of enough facilities

10. a. My school is covering all l think should be done
    ☐ Yes   ☐ No
    b. If your response to 10. a. is No, state the aspects you wish were Covered which are not being covered.
    (a). _____
    (b). _____
    (c). _____

11. In my opinion the factors that promote high performance in students are:
    ☐ Committed teachers
    ☐ Hard working students
    ☐ Availability of textbooks
    ☐ Science laboratory
    ☐ Good library
    ☐ All of the above

12. In your opinion, what incentives would impress teachers and staff of a school in order to perform to their highest level.
    ☐ Good and attractive remuneration
    ☐ Better housing accommodation
    ☐ Attractive benefits and allowance
    ☐ Motivation and staff development
    Other factors:
        a. ....
        b. ....

13. Leadership/ Administration at your school is:
    ☐ Doing what is supposed to do
    ☐ Does not address the needs of the students and staff
    ☐ It is autocratic in nature
    ☐ It is democratic in nature
    ☐ It is running the school smoothly
    ☐ Do not know
    Other comments:
        1. ....
        2. ....

14. a. If the government could privatize all secondary schools in Zimbabwe, would it improve performance? Tick
    ☐ Yes   ☐ No
    b. If yes: what could be improved?
    ☐ Facilities of the school
    ☐ Teaching methods
    ☐ Quality of learning
    ☐ The results of the students
    Other views:
        1. ....
        2. ....

15. In private school, sports activities are a priority as well as academic
    - ☐ Yes   ☐ No
    - ☐ Strongly agree
    - ☐ Agree
    - ☐ Disagree
    - ☐ Strongly disagree

16. From my observation, students at my school have adopted the following habits (Tick as many are applicable)
    - ☐ Reading habit
    - ☐ Have adopted the study group culture
    - ☐ Prefer art subjects than science subjects
    - ☐ Tolerate the teachers who do not come for duty

17. a. Both the staff and students know the ways to perform to their full capacity
    - ☐ Yes   ☐ No

    b. Know but can't communicate with the administration
    - ☐ They fear to be victimized
    - ☐ The administration is not friendly
    Other comments:
    1. ....
    2. ....

18. Private schools have better teachers and better facilities to enhance education.
    What do you say about this view?
    - ☐ This is true to a great extent
    - ☐ They have better facilities but good teachers
    - ☐ The facilities in a school enhance better performance
    - ☐ All schools are the same
    Other comments:
    a. ....
    b. ....
    c. ....

19. The reasons why some students fail their 'O' levels and 'A' levels is because
    ☐ The type of school they are in
    ☐ Lack of proper learning
    ☐ No motivation from their teachers
    ☐ Leadership styles in public school does not promote learning environment

20. Public / government schools do not have democratic leadership in nature
    ☐ I agree strongly
    ☐ I disagree
    ☐ Some of them have
    ☐ All of them have
    ☐ All of them are autocratic
    ☐ Their administration does not have vision

21. Non-academic staff contribute on the success or failure of students in their performance on their results.
    ☐ They do not contribute
    ☐ They do contribute
    ☐ The school need both teaching staff and non-teaching staff
    ☐ The school flourishes if all work together
    Other comments:
        a. ....
        b. ....

22. The government should not control the curriculum instead they should allow the private schools to contribute also
    (Tick as many as are applicable)
    ☐ I agree totally
    ☐ I do not agree
    ☐ I agree to some extent
    ☐ Government is having monopoly in Education

Other reasons why:
a. ....
b. ....

23. The public schools do not have efficiency, effectiveness and competency compared to private schools.
☐ Not true
☐ True
☐ 90% true
☐ 50% true

24. All schools in Zimbabwe must be controlled by the government, the ministry of Education
☐ Yes ☐ No
If yes, why and how?
a. ....
b. ....

25. Leadership styles/ Administration in both private and public schools must be evaluated yearly by the Ministry of Education
☐ I strongly agree
☐ Not wise, let private schools be autonomous
☐ Government's supervision is very poo

APPENDIX II

Interviews of students and staff

1. Who chose the school for you, your parents or yourself?
2. If it were your choice, would you choose private or public school?
3. What do you like most in your school?
4. Are the teachers at your school active in terms of teaching relevant education?
5. Do you know the pass rate of your school among other schools in your district?
6. Which level has always the highest pass rate, 'O' level or 'A' level?
7. How many lessons do you have per week?
8. What would you say are the major delivery strategies used in Education at your school?
9. Who is responsible for your school fees?
10. Do you think the education system applied at your school is relevant for your future?
11. What leadership style do you think your school have? Autocratic or democratic?
12. Is the administration at your school good enough to address your problems?
13. Is any good rapport between student and staff and staff to staff?
14. How would you rate your administration: a very good b. poor c. very poor d. moderate?
15. How would you say are the conditions of service: an excellence b. very poor c. poor d. satisfactory?

16. If you were given a choice, would you choose your school again for your education?
17. Are the students having satisfactory discipline to foster conducive and learning environment?
18. What are your suggestions to improve the performance, results and good discipline in your school?
19. Can the Ministry of Education privatize all the education system in Zimbabwe?
20. Whom would you say is responsible for performance in improving results of 'O' level and 'A' level in your schools? Students or staff? Give reasons.
21. Are the facilities adequate in your school to promote progress in performance?
22. Are the teachers having adequate incentives and benefits to motivate them to enjoy their work, according to observations?
23. Does work promote sporting?
24. Can you recommend any one to come at your school

BIBLIOGRAPHY/ REFERENCES

Avalos, B. (1991), Approaches to teacher Evaluation Initial Teacher Training, London, Commonwealth Secretariat.

Borg, W.R. and Gall, M.D (1983), Education Research; An Introduction, Longman, New York.

Dalin, P. (1994), How Schools Improve, London, Imtec Publishers.

Datta, A. (1984), Education and Society: A sociology Of Africa Education, London Macmillan.

Day, C (1999), Developing Teachers, London, Falmer Press.

Hunter, P. (1998), Developing Education, London, PC (Pvt) Ltd Publishers.

Isaac, S. Michael W.B. (1984), Handbook in Research and Evaluation, Edits, San Diego.

Kemmer, F. (1994), Utilizing Education and Human Resources Sector Analyses, Paris ENESCO Publishers

Leedy, P.C (1980), Practical Research Planning and Design, MacMillan Publishers, New York.

Levine, V. (1996), The Economics and Finance of Education in Zimbabwe, May 1996, Harare, UNICEF Press

MacMillan, J.H and Schumacher, S (1993), Research in Education A Conceptual Introduction.

Marshall, T. (1991), Understanding Leadership, London, Macmillan Press.

Mbamba, A. (1992), Handbook on Training Methods in Educational Management, Harare UNESCO

McMahonn W. and Geske T (1982), Financing Education: Overcoming Inefficiency and Inequity, Urbana, University of Illinois Press

63

Mugodzwa, T (1999), <u>An Investigation into the factors that Negatively impacted on the Academic performance of 'O' Level Students in rural day secondary Schools in Mhondoro – Ngezi, Kadoma District:1990 to 1998</u>, not Published, UZ Library.

Nelson, J, Carlson K, and Palonsky S. (1996), <u>Critical Issues in Education</u>, New York, McGraw-Hill Publishers.

Nyawaranda, V. (1998), <u>Teachers Beliefs About teaching English as a second language (ESL): Two case studies of ESL Instruction in Zimbabwe</u>, Not published, UZ Library.

Pole C and Chawla – Duggan, (1996), <u>Reshaping Education in 1990:</u> Perspectives <u>on secondary</u> Schooling, London, Falmer Press.

Pilot, D and Hungler, P. (1987), <u>Practical Research: An Introduction</u>, London, Longman.

Rebone, R (1991), <u>Personnel Administration in Education</u>, Boston, Allyn and Bacon Publishers.

Stenhouse, L.C (1975), <u>An Introduction to Curriculum Research and Development,</u> Oxford, Heinemann Publishers.

Tobin, D (1996), <u>Transformational Learning</u>, New York, John Wiley and Sons Publishers.

Vos A. J and Brits (1990), <u>Comparative Education and National Education System</u>, Durban, Butterworths.

Watkins, K (2000), <u>The Oxfam Education Report</u>, London, Oxfam GB

Wincharuck, P (1988), <u>Building Effective Leadership</u>, Washington DC, Heinemann Publishers.

<u>https://www.fatherly.com/love-money/private-schools-vs-private-schools-facts-benefits-statistics/Accessed</u> November, 23, 2020.

Printed in the United States
by Baker & Taylor Publisher Services